the

Panty Dropper
COOKBOOK

IF YOU ARE A

WOMAN

CLOSE THIS BOOK

NOW!

YOU WON'T FIND THIS BOOK

ON OPRAH'S BOOK LIST.

IF YOU ARE A WOMAN,

CLOSE THIS BOOK

NOW!

The Panty Dropper Cookbook
by Sam Dodge

Dedicated To All Young Men

Life's uncertain.
Ride your best horse first.

Illustrations by Helen Dodge

This is a new type of book.

It's a 21st century book.

The Panty Dropper Cookbook
is 80% book & 20% web site.

It's a blend of paper and ink and virtual reality.

ISBN Number 978-0-9820636-0-6

THIS BOOK SHOULD WIN A PULITZER

You will never see this book nominated for a Pulitzer Prize.

It should be nominated and it should win, but the men who run the Pulitzer committee are all afraid of the women in their lives.

If you are a woman, close this book now!

You won't find this book nominated for a Nobel Prize in literature either, though it should be. Many men are going to find this the most poignant and influential book they have ever read.

If you are a woman and you have read this far, you are cheating. Close this book now or buy it for a young man you know and love.

Table of Contents

The Core Mating Drive Of The Male 8

Uncomfortable Asking For A Date? 10

Not Enough Dates? Not Enough Sex? 11

The Gate Guardians 13

Comfort Zones 14

The Invite To Dinner 17

Porn. I'm Not Kidding. 18

Chocolate Is A Panty Dropper 20

Wine and Alcohol 22

Cleaning Up 24

Don't Ever 25

Instructions 27

Your Kitchen and Supplies 28

Cooking Basics and Beyond 31

Breakfast In Bed 38

Penis-Shaped Foods 40

If You Are Under Thirty 42

Thoughts and Advice 43

THE RECIPES 49

    Caprese Salad 54

    Boiled Artichokes with Lemon-Garlic Butter 56

    Bacon-Wrapped Scallops with Jasmine Rice
        & Baby Spinach Greens 58

    Spicy Shrimp and Mesclun Greens 60

    Seared Pork Tenderloin with Roasted Red Potatoes
        & Tomato Wine Butter Sauce 62

    Chicken with Couscous & Broccoli 64

    Filet Mignon with Garlic Mashers,
        Green Beans & Sauce Verde .66

    Chicken, Seafood & Bacon Paella 70

    Pasta with Pesto, Sautéed Mushrooms,
        Fresh Tomatoes & Artichoke Hearts 72

    Chocolate Icebox Cake 74

    Chile Cheese Egg Dish 76

Thanks 79

The Core Mating Drive Of The Male

Every woman has two breasts. Women comprise just over 50% of the world's population. This means there are more than twice as many breasts on the planet than there are men. I don't even know why I brought this up. It's a cool visual though.

A note on dealing with the core mating drive of the human male: A man thinks about sex every ten minutes, maybe more. I have to say I don't think this fine point in the male brain has changed for thousands

of years. If anything, the sex drive might have intensified.

This book, as well as being a cookbook, tells young men to go hunting for a prize. The "prize" is what's in a girl's panties.

the

COOKBOOK

This isn't really a cookbook. This is a book about hunting.

I can't imagine that the title of this cookbook will grant me an interview on any major network TV talk show. I have thought about changing the name of the book so I could promote it on talk shows. *First Date Cookbook* came to mind. After sampling all of the meals in the book and doing some focused research, I have to stay loyal to the book's original name. *The Panty Dropper Cookbook* won't get me on Oprah, but again, you guys don't watch Oprah anyway.

The idea behind this book is to help single guys get comfortable in their relationships with women. It's not about finding the right woman to spend eternity with. It's about finding the right woman to spend the night with. It's about getting comfortable being alone with the woman who leaves her panties on your bedroom floor.

This is not some historical romance novel. I promise not to drive you to the dictionary. It's a simple book targeted at a simple project. If, however, you do have to look up a single word I've written here, I think the whole world would appreciate it if you would please start the next week with a vasectomy. Really, you probably shouldn't reproduce with another human if you find yourself looking up any word in this book.

This book comes with a very serious warning. "I lost all my magic powers right after I got married!" This happens to almost all men. Just ask any man about it.

All men are born with magic powers. Ask a man when he thinks he lost them. He'll say it was just after he got married. Here is the one caveat: You can only ask this question when he is not in the presence of his wife, or he will lie.

Uncomfortable Asking For A Date?

This book is designed to take the edge off the hard part of dating. Dating is part of growing up for most Americans, and for guys it is a must. Guys get most of their sexual experiences from dating, and the more practice they get, the better. When the time comes and they find a girl they really want to impress, good sexual know-how is at the top of the list. Remember, a girl likes a guy with confidence. Knowing about good sexual practices will give you more confidence, and more confidence leads to more girls, more dates and more sex.

Women like to think that we are interested in them; interested in their personalities, in their character, and who they are. Show them you care and they will be intrigued. From a woman's point of view, all other women have the same furry toy in their panties that they do. So they think, *"What's the big deal?"*

The politically correct women are going to think this book is telling you to objectify women. That's not true. The book is telling you to learn how truly wonderful women are. Objectify what they keep in their panties.

Thirty percent of men wouldn't approach "Miss Perfect" if she were across the room. It's because the man doesn't know what to say after *"Hello, how are you? My name is…"* What's the opening "date" line?

Well, how about this simple solution: *"I'm working on a dinner recipe and I'd like your opinion. Can I make it for you?"* She might ask if you're asking her out on a date, and before you start thinking about it, just say, *"Yes!"* She'll most likely say yes right away too. Chances are, you both want a date anyway. If she rejects your offer, move on; it's not about you. Don't take it personally. You'll get rejections, we all do, even girls. You can handle it.

Not Enough Dates? Not Enough Sex?

Has another month gone by without those empty panties visiting your bedroom floor? Do you have a problem? Having not been well defined, it might not have appeared as a problem to you, and there wouldn't have been much of a solution to it anyway. However, using this cookbook to create an inviting environment with good food and wine for the lady of your choice, you will surely make a vast improvement to your overnight guest list.

Panty dropping! Guys, WTF, this ain't rocket surgery. Like most goals, it takes some preparation. It's a hunting process. As American men, we don't hunt much anymore. In the past, no hunter simply walked out on the porch and had ducks fall from the sky. He had to prepare for the hunt, and the same applies here and now. Preparation is what works.

Preparation

On these pages you'll learn how to entice a woman to your place with a great meal. You'll learn what to buy to create it and how to prepare it to get the pleasures you are hunting for—*before, during and especially after* the meal. Preparation is no more than the task of preparing the right atmosphere and simple, easy meals that induce ease and relaxation and the eventual "panty drop." Most of these meals are designed for the most inept bachelor to be able to cook. Some are a little more sophisticated. Once you get good at preparing "panty dropping" meals, you can move up. None of the meals in this book are difficult. Find your own pace with them, practice and have a good time. Remember the goal. You are on a hunt. Stay focused.

Your first impression and opening dialogue are very important. What you say and how you say it are the first steps. Here are a few things you must know about what girls like.

The Gate Guardians

Women have primitive and ancient sexual "gates" you have to pass through. They keep her from mating with just anybody and everybody. These are put into place by the gate guardians that you as a male don't have.

Our part in the mating dance is to indiscriminately scatter semen across the countryside. We have the mating brain of a bird.

The women's version of the 'mating brain of a bird' has some criteria that must be met. You'll need to know how to please the gate guardians so they will give you a pass to get on with the sex part. Remember the prize. Owning that furry warm thing in her panties.

Once she's at your house, you don't have to be a genius in order to get those panties to the floor. Serving her a good meal with good wine, paying her the compliment of being in service to her, will draw down those panties faster than you can imagine. Now, differentiate here. Being in service doesn't mean being a servant. Being served by a servant isn't interesting, but a man *being in service* to a woman is very sexy to her.

Remember this about dating. If you are uncomfortable asking for a date, you are not alone. Several million men feel uncomfortable asking for a date. Nearly sixty-eight percent of men are reluctant to ask a woman out because, as you know, it's not easy. The fear of rejection is very real and inhibiting.

Comfort Zones

We all try to live within our comfort zone. When we get outside our comfort zone, we get uneasy, and getting too far away from it, we'll even break into a sweat. Here's a short example of comfort zone uneasiness. Lets say you are driving the speed limit along with many other cars on the freeway. How uncomfortable are you going to be with a cop behind you and not behind anyone else?

If you find yourself being uncomfortable on a daily basis, your comfort zone is too tight. You need to make it taller or wider. Once you've learned the tricks to giving yourself more room, you'll find living easier and less stressful. Your confidence will go up and it'll show in everything you do. This is probably one of the single most effective changes for the better you can make in your life.

If you're like most people, you have areas of self-doubt. We all do. Women do too. These self-doubt issues mean very little to the rest of the world. They are just self-limiting issues that your brain uses to keep you within your comfort zone.

Being naked with a woman might mean you are going to be outside your comfort zone. Yet being naked with a woman *is* the goal!

Think of your self-doubts. Is she really going to notice those things about you that make you insecure? They are not going to mean to her what they mean to you. Do you think she will notice your imperfections?

She'll be too concerned with her own to even notice yours. Most of the time, if she does notice that you have six toes, she's not going to care anyway. Step out of that circle of doubt and get on with your goal!

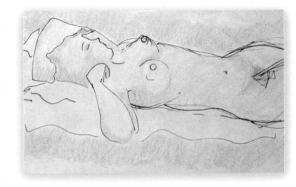

Remember that she's nervous too. Her doubts are going to be about how attractive you think she is. She's interested in attracting a mate, but she's afraid you'll notice that her butt's too big, one tit's bigger than the other or that she's got one blue eye and one brown eye (just kidding). Even professional models have concerns about their own imperfections. The point is, we all have self-doubts. Learning to ignore them will help get you into bed with a naked woman, more often than not.

Uncertainty is with us all. It can cause fear. It inhibits us and causes us NOT to act on our desires. Work your way through the fear. Push the edges of your comfort zone. You are not alone, everyone is afraid at times. Everyone has failures. It's OK to fail, but it's not OK to give up before you start.

Defense and escape mechanisms work when you want to get away from a life-threatening situation. Luckily, the need doesn't come up too often in today's society. When was the last time you had to escape from something that was going to kill you and eat you? Unless you live in New Jersey, I can't imagine the 'fight or flight' defense having been of much use to you in the past month or so.

When you ask a girl over for dinner and she says yes, I guarantee you that she's fantasizing about the same romantic evening ending in sexual pleasure that you're fantasizing about. Help her out. Ask her to dinner at your place and then make her fantasy come true.

"I'm working on a new recipe. I'd like to make it for you and have you give me your opinion." What's the best thing that can happen? Pleasured animal noises behind closed doors and some much-needed exercise.

What's the worst thing that can happen? She might say, "no."
Then you have single sex again. Let's face it, unless you are Catholic, you have had more single sex than the other kind anyway. You should be really good at it by now. So where's the down side?

Once you think it through and understand the realities of the fear problem, it'll be an easy 'work-around.'

The Invite To Dinner

Invite a girl to come have dinner with you *in your home*. By bringing a girl over to have a great dinner with you, you've eliminated that dreaded question, "Your place or mine?" Half the battle is already won.

In the "dinner out" scenario, all you have done is buy the meal. You have tried good conversation, but it has been repeatedly interrupted by the wait staff. Any attempt at intimacy is impossible. The question *"Would you like to come over for a nightcap?"* is a loaded question, and could mean many things:

1. *Do you like me enough to come over to my place?*

2. *Should I have spent more money?*

3. *Did I spend enough on dinner to make you think I value you enough that you'll spend the night?*

4. *Was dinner enough, or do we have to go dancing before you reject me?*

5. *How stupid do I feel having lead myself into this trap?*

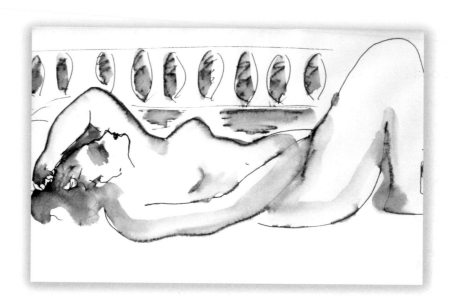

Porn. I'm Not Kidding.

Cooking *IS* porn for women. I'm not kidding. To a woman, the result of having a man cook a meal for her is very much like great porn is to a man. Watching a man be in service and cooking for her will make her wet. It's a wonderfully slow rise for her. Women like a slow arousal, about ten times as slow as a man. Cook for her using the techniques contained in this book and I'll bet that there will be some evenings when you end up in bed before you are finished with the meal.

From nothing, on a surprise, a man can be ready for sex in less than half a minute. And be finished in less than three. Not a woman. She wants her sexual experience to be long and slow. Remember, she is coming to the dinner with thoughts of romance. You are coming to the dinner with thoughts of sex. You are catering to her romantic expectations by wining and dining her in your home. Romance is emotional while sex is physical. Can you satisfy both? Absolutely. You have the responsibility to yourself to make sure the evening goes so well that when you wake up the next morning, there's an empty pair of panties on your bedroom floor. If she has a willing girlfriend, you might even end up with two empty pairs of panties on your bedroom floor.

This book will lead to better sex for you. If you aren't getting enough action now, (and who is?) this book should really improve your sex life. Good food and drink doesn't often fail.

The idea here is to have you be in control of the evening. Women love that. You don't have to be a control freak, just lead her on a romantic path that starts in the kitchen and ends up in the bedroom. You take care of her in the kitchen and she'll take care of you in the bedroom. She'll want to please you. Expect tons of heavy breathing and if she's a screamer, you can expect congratulations from your neighbors next time you see them.

She's going to want to tell her girlfriends about her night out with you. They're all going to know that she spent the night. They aren't going to care about that part of the story. What they want to hear is what romantic things you did to get her to give herself to you. Do a good job and

you're likely to have one of her friends over for dinner next month. Which one? You'll get a hint when she mentions she heard that you can cook. Invite her over to get her opinion. I'm not kidding, they'll talk and another one will be over soon.

Chocolate Is A Panty Dropper

"I love chocolate. Do you like chocolate?"

This could easily be the best opening line you could possibly use.

"Tell me a little about yourself. Do you prefer to be on top?"

The chocolate line works, while the other works about one percent of the time. The odds say you have to use it a hundred times to get laid once. If you have ever used this line, you have a very close relationship with your right hand and you probably don't need this book.

Chocolate isn't so innocent. She knows it, but probably won't think you know it. Serve chocolate-dipped strawberries and you'll have a chance to find out what kind of sound panties make when hitting the floor.

The key here is "fresh" strawberries and high-end sweet chocolate. Be sure the strawberries have the stem or "handle" still on them. Keep the chocolate warm and fluid by placing it in a pan over hot water. Place a luscious strawberry into her mouth. When you see her put a chocolate-dipped strawberry to her lips, you'll barely be able to keep control of the dragon in your shorts.

> *"Twill make old women young and fresh,*
>
> *Create new motions of the flesh.*
>
> *And cause them long for you know what,*
>
> *If they but taste of chocolate."*
>
> –James Wadworth, 1768-1844
> *A History of the Nature and Quality of Chocolate*

Act interested, dummy. At this point I know what part of her you are thinking about, but it's too soon. Patience. Those cute little frilly things will be on the floor in a short while.

How decadent does she feel? If she professes to be a true chocoholic, there could be an after-meal dessert in store for you. Explore the possibilities. There is a really great body chocolate out there. Yup, I said, "body chocolate." It comes in a small jar complete with a paintbrush. Nipple painting could be in order tonight.

One caveat: It has to be a new jar and a new paintbrush for every date. She won't want to think she's been second or third on the brush.

> *Self-discipline implies some unpleasant things to me, including staying away from chocolate and keeping my hands out of women's pants.*
> –Oleg Kiselev

> *Researchers have discovered that chocolate produced some of the same reactions in the brain as marijuana. The researchers also discovered other similarities between the two, but can't remember what they are.*
> –Author Unknown

Wine and Alcohol

Remember the goal here: *Panties on the floor.* Alcohol dulls the gate guardians and loosens a girl's inhibitions. That's a good thing. Wine is expected and it's an important part of a good meal.

If there is a winery in your neighborhood, that's a good starting place. Wineries are great for learning about what wine goes with what food. Visit a local winery and ask questions, then go with what you like. If you like the wine, chances are she'll like it too. Tell her about how you chose the wine you're having for her special dinner. If there isn't a winery in your area, go to a wine shop. They're great at recommending a choice for you, and you can usually find better prices than at a winery.

You can usually get great wines at your local grocery store. Any shopper will gladly advise you.

In general, a good white wine will go with chicken, fish or salad, and a good red will go with meats, stews and soups.

Get a good crusty bread and some cheese to serve before the meal no matter what wine you chose.

Pinot Grigio and Chardonnay are today's most popular white wines. Serve them chilled. Cabernet Sauvignon or a Merlot will be good choices for your reds. Serve reds at room temperature.

Have both red and white wine ready at your dinner. Ask her what she'd prefer. Wine will help her relax and help raise her testosterone level. Elevated testosterone means elevated mating desire.

In most of Europe, a wearable prescription testosterone patch is now available to help raise the testosterone level in women. It's very popular. It seems like women want more sex.

Wine is a great aphrodisiac for women. Your good wine will help them get all the sex they could possibly want. The testosterone patch won't be available here for many years. Too bad.

Serve your wine in glasses made of real glass. Never serve it in plastic glasses. Wine in plastic glasses is like serving Filet Mignon on a paper plate.

Ten dollars should buy you good wine. Fill her glass a couple of times, but don't let either of you get drunk. Your adventure will come to a screeching halt if you do. Sex is no good when you're drunk.
The party will be over. Have just one bottle. It will be plenty, as you both want to remember the pleasure of the night.

The morning can be just as good as the night before. You should be looking forward to a repeat performance. Morning sex is great. However, if she doesn't remember the night before, she might be inclined to run off first thing. No breakfast and no repeat performance. Not only is this not good for morning seconds, it's probably not good for another date with her either.

If you bring a woman home from a night of drinking out, be careful of the "oops" syndrome. You drank too much the night before. You wake up in the morning and there's a large permanent dent in your bed. Who or what did you bring home? Finding a Kong-sized pair of panties in your room is never comfortable unless you're a *Chubby Chaser*. What were you thinking? If your bed is empty and her giant-size UNDERPANTS are still on the floor, you'll find her in your refrigerator.

Cleaning Up

Clean your place the day before she comes over. Clean it again before you start prepping your meal. Clean your kitchen and clean your bathroom. Ladies like clean. They see dirt most guys don't see or care about. I'm not saying that you should be anal about cleaning. That would put a negative spin on things for a single guy. Just clean your place up and make it look sanitary. We've all seen a single guy's place that looks like it could be an evil scientist's experiment gone bad. Sanitary is the optimum word here. Women would like to be able to touch anything in your place without feeling contaminated. If they perceive your place as being clean, they'll perceive you as being clean. Splurge on some flowers. Pop them in a vase or even a glass. Put them where she's sure to see them. Make it "nice." This will have her feel better about letting you touch her hidden fur.

Clean up the kitchen as you go. In many cases you will have three or four minutes of idle time while cooking the entree to the meal. Just wash a couple of things you have already used. When you are finished, there won't be much cleanup to take time away from the bedroom. Remember, you might want to serve breakfast to her the following morning. She will be impressed that you don't leave dirty items sitting in the sink overnight. Believe it or not, cleaning as you go is very attractive.

If you are lucky enough to have a dishwasher, be sure to fill it and run it right after the meal. Having no items with food on them left in the sink overnight will help get you a return visit.

Clean your bathroom. This is the last place she will visit before your bed. You don't want to take the edge off what is coming. Remember, she

might take a casual look in the bathroom drawers while she's in there. Keep them tidy. Have the toilet lid down before she arrives. Really, I'm not kidding, lid down. No man truly understands the toilet lid thing. Never mind, just put it down.

Don't Ever

Don't ever cook a meal for her that takes too long to prepare. The recipes in this book are all designed to be 30 minutes or less for a reason. You don't want to look like you are really good at domestic stuff. If you make yourself a chef and cook for two hours, she'll be thinking to herself, "Does he sew too?!" Remember, she may be looking for a wife. Keeping the kitchen time to a minimum means you can spend more time with your favorite furry pet. Remember what the evening is really about.

DON'T EVER talk politics or religion, and DON'T EVER mention exes. Ever!

Politics has no place in the bedroom. It's a sure bet when discussing politics, one of you will be in the wrong. As always, with this subject, it's a matter of ego. You both want to be right. As long as she's wrong, her panties will stay put.

Religion! Dear Jesus! This could be a real problem. If she's really religious her panties are being held up by faith. You don't have a chance. I think here I have exceeded the authority of the Politically Correct Police and moved into the realm of the Religious Police. The Religious Police are more threatening than the PC police. The severely Christian RP actually scare me.

Once again, exes are a big turn off. Never[2] mention an ex. 'Nuf said.

DON'T EVER make chili and think it's going to be a panty dropper. It's a guy's food. There is no recipe for chili in this book. It's for the Sunday TV football game with the guys. It's the beans—spicy hot, the onions, the potential gas, plus the pure bulk of chili that make it a non-panty dropper meal. No kidding. Make chili; sleep alone tonight. Women want to eat light before sex.

DON'T EVER serve asparagus.

Asparagus is out, all the way out. Asparagus has some sulfur-containing amino acids. About 50% of humans have a chemical in their digestive systems that causes a breakdown of this sulfur and they excrete it in their urine. Shortly after eating asparagus, your pee can smell really bad. It's the same type of sulfur that makes skunks smell bad. You have a 50-50 chance of having this reaction and so does she. I'm not good with low math, but two people with a 50-50 chance sounds like 100% asparagus odor to me. The breakdown of the sulfur happens almost immediately. Follow this "Don't Ever" hint and you won't have an asparagus-flavored after-meal meal.

DON'T EVER serve anything with MSG in it.

MSG (Monosodium Glutamate) gives some people headaches. You can't afford to take that chance. Your evening isn't going to be successful if you invite her over and then give her a headache.

"Not tonight honey, I have a headache" is no joke. Women's blood pressure rises when they get sexually aroused. Higher blood pressure will increase her headache. Any level headache equals no sex. Remember, you are stalking something she has in her possession. She's more likely to let you play with it if she doesn't have a headache.

DON'T EVER be late to your own dinner.

She'll think you don't really care about her. Maybe you don't, but her panties will only come off if she thinks you care about HER. She wants to believe that you want to "make love to her." That means paying attention to the part of her that's opposite to where the panties sit. Paying attention to her face and her eyes is important. What she thinks you think about her is very important. She knows all guys are willing to go for what she has in her panties. Do what you think will make her happy and you'll be rewarded. Keep your eyes on the goal.

Instructions

To be used once her panties are off.

This actually is a cookbook, so I won't give you instructions on what to do once her panties and bra are off. For those instructions, you need to go to one of the self-help books or web sites. Maybe I don't mean "self help." Being a guy, you already know all you'll ever know or need to know about "self help."

This book is about that part of the evening before her panties hit the floor. If you've ever imagined being a rock star, movie star, Broadway star, TV star—in short, any type of performing star—this is your chance. You have a performance to put on the night she comes to dinner.

A talent show. It can't be transparent, so you have to be yourself and in character the whole evening. The entire act is about self-confidence, and putting on your best self. Nothing more. It'll work. Remember, you CAN be a great turn-on for women.

Watch the videos on our web site on how to handle the kitchen utensils. Practice. It doesn't take much time to get really good with a kitchen knife. She'll love your hands. She'll be thinking about your hands and what they can do for her.

Eye contact

Don't look at her breasts or her crotch. Look into her eyes. Women wonder why men look at their breasts. If men aren't looking there, they'll be looking at her crotch. Women know men are just breeding animals, driven by "the small head."

If she runs into a guy who looks into her eyes, she will think the guy is interested in her more than the other two parts. That's intriguing for her. She will want you to make love to her. Look into her eyes.

Your Kitchen and Supplies

If you already have a good supply of kitchen utensils you can just glance through this chapter to see if you can use an upgrade to your kitchen.

I promise I won't try to sell you on a handcrafted Italian bottle brush. This chapter should be simple and uncluttered. Some of the items will be a little spendy, but I have personally used and tested most. I want you to be comfortable with the tools you are going to use. Sometimes

cheap just looks cheap and there is only one way around it. I won't recommend high-end, very costly items, if a lesser, inexpensive one will do just as well. For the research on this book, I have purchased both and used both. I recommend what works. I don't believe in form over function. It can look modern, even futuristic, but if it doesn't work for what you want, what good is it? Easy-to-use tools will make you look like a star.

TOOLS YOU'LL NEED

With careful shopping, you can buy your items online or from stores like Target, which have very good kitchen and household departments and are not too pricey.

Non-Stick Saucepans and Frying Pans

Buy Teflon-coated saucepans and frying pans with lids. This is for your benefit. Easy to wash and food won't stick to them. Also, the food will look presentable when you serve it. What you serve to her has to have a 'look' to it. It will get you past one of her gate guardians. Let's face it, if you were home alone, you'd eat any mess out of a frying pan while standing at the stove. You've done it before, haven't you?

Here are the simple rules to keeping your Teflon healthy:
Never use metal utensils with Teflon. Wood or plastic will do very well.

Always have oil or liquid in the pan when you bring it up to heat, and bring it up slowly. Don't put a pan on high heat. Instead, put the pan on the cold burner and then bring up the heat.

Make sure your saucepans have well-fitting lids. You will need saucepans in which to make sauces, soups, rice, and in a large pot, pasta. Buy pots and pans with a good look to them so that you look like a pro when they're out on the counter. If your recipe calls for a lid and you don't have one, use the lid of a large pot.

Pot for Pasta:
You will need a large pot with a lid.

Pyrex Baking Dish
Have at least one 13×9×2" Pyrex baking dish

Knives
Have good knives. These are very important and will make your work much easier. Knives dull easily when they're rattling around in a drawer, so keep them in a wood knife block. Most chefs only use about three knives. Buy a small wood knife block to keep your cooking knives on the counter and out of a drawer. You'll need a large, sharp knife for cutting and dicing your vegetables. You'll need a smaller paring knife for finer, more detailed work like cutting up apples and cheese, and you'll need a serrated bread knife. Sharp knives are safer on your fingers because you don't have to push as hard and the food won't slip. Watch the prep videos at *thepantydroppercookbook.com*.

Timer
A kitchen timer is a necessity. Your kitchen stove will have a built-in timer, but buy a portable one anyway. Get an easy-to-read, loud kitchen timer. You don't want to undercook or overcook anything. There is a small range of tolerance to overcooking or undercooking your food. Try to stay within the cooking range indicated. A timer will also help you stay focused on the meal instead of being distracted by a Beaver. *Can you still call it a Beaver if it's shaved?* (Just a thought.)

Measuring spoons and cups

When a recipe calls for a measurement, try to accurately measure. Once you get used to making that particular recipe, you can add and subtract things according to your own taste. Measuring spoons are inexpensive and usually come on a metal ring so they all stay together. Only use metal ones. Skip plastic altogether. OXO brand products have a great look and really work well for what they're supposed to do.

Glass and metal measuring cups don't cost much, and are a must in your kitchen. Glass measuring cups are for liquid and the metal ones are for dry ingredients like flour and sugar. Buy some that look nice and modern. You don't want to look like you're using stuff you inherited from your grandmother. Once again, OXO brand products have a nice look and are extremely functional.

Tongs

You'll need tongs to turn things over in the frying pan. Get metal ones with plastic tips so they won't scratch the non-stick coating on your pans.

A pinch

Actually, there are two sizes for a "pinch:" a two-finger pinch and a three-finger pinch… count your thumb as one of the fingers. DUH. I don't want to demean any of you, but you mustn't overthink this book. Remember, it's for "the mating brain of a bird." Cooking is very simple, and let's keep it that way.

Cooking Basics and Beyond

Cooking really is simple. You are simply heating things up and making them taste better. The simpler I can make this task for you the better. You can do this. The result will be that she'll love you for it. Here are some of the basics you will need to know and to have. You will want to have some things, like spices, salt and pepper, olive oil and vinegar, always in your cupboard. I have prepared a general list for you. With this list you can do almost anything.

*Grains of Paradise
with its own grinder*
A little pricey, but you'll love this spice as it comes with a story that you can tell offhand. She'll love the story and the spice. Grains of Paradise are used in a pepper grinder and is used instead of regular black pepper. It's not an acquired taste, it's a great new taste. Have two pepper grinders on the table. One regular old grinder and one really nice one. Fill the nice one with Grains of Paradise. It is an interesting spice as it changes flavor with the food you use it on.

Good for a laugh at dinner:
Grains of Paradise was an extremely trendy spice in the Middle Ages. Not only was it used as a spice but as protection from being attacked by spells from witches. So, you can ask her if she has a problem with any of the local witches and tell her you and your Grains of Paradise are going to protect her tonight. (It kind of suggests a Knight in Shining Armor, romance novels, panties on the floor, etc.) You may or may not want to tell her in the morning that it also is used in spells to promote lust.

Seasonings

When selecting your store-bought seasonings, wherever you can, select ones that are salt-free. Otherwise you'll need to remember to compensate when adding salt to taste. It's always better to have too little salt than too much. Tell her you've made the meal low in salt so she can season it to her taste. Once again, it will appear you are thinking of her. Panties are slipping lower!

Too much salt threatens to put you into a restaurant for your panty-dropping meal. This ain't good, guys. Going out defeats the purpose. She'll have been so close to your bedroom, and now you've had to self-eject from potential paradise. Keep the salt low and let her season to her taste.

With today's economy, you really want her to be at your house. My guess is that with a matchup of meal for meal, the recipes in this book and on the web site will cost you about one third of what they would in a restaurant.

The following is a list that you should have on hand.
Dried ingredients last a long time. Buy fresh ingredients often.

1. Sea salt or kosher salt
2. Pepper
3. Roasted red peppers (can or jar)
4. Herbes de Provence (parsley, rosemary, thyme)
5. Fresh onions
6. Fresh garlic
7. Tiger Sauce®
8. Soy sauce
9. Green Tabasco® (milder with more flavor)
10. Honey
11. Heavy whipping cream (make sure it's fresh)
12. Chicken broth
13. Extra virgin olive oil
14. Garlic powder
15. Rice (jasmine and arborio)
16. Teriyaki sauce
17. Morton® Nature's Seasons®
18. Salt-free lemon and herb seasoning
19. Pasta (penne, linguini, angel hair)
20. Eggs
21. All-purpose flour
22. Butter (make sure it's fresh)
23. Wine, red and white
24. Chocolate
25. Grains of Paradise

MEATS

Chicken is easy and good. Skinless, boneless chicken breasts are available in the meat department of every supermarket. They freeze well. Just remember to bring chicken from the freezer to your refrigerator a full day before you plan on cooking it. If you have a microwave oven you can always use it to defrost your foods too.

If you are going to serve a steak, remember your portion has to be equal to hers. If you want a big steak, you had better think of having it another night, and think about eating it alone or with the guys.

She is going to want something around six or eight ounces. She wants the most tender piece of meat made by God. She doesn't want to chew and chew in front of a potential mate. Give her a break. Buy the best quality there is.

Buy from a professional meat cutter. Tell him what small size you want AND WHY YOU WANT IT. Don't be embarrassed. Tell him you want an aged piece of beef so tender and flavorful she'll drop 'em right at the dinner table. He'll be excited to find you the best piece of meat he has. He wants to help you be successful in your hunt. He also wants to hear the outcome next time you are in his shop. Remember, ALL men are on your side. If there is anything we can do to help get her panties on the floor, we'll do it. Don't be afraid to ask any of the male food suppliers for help. Don't forget to tell them how successful their help made your evening. Tell them about this book and where they can get one for themselves.

The steak needs to look good and be an even thickness all the way around. You don't want any part to cook more than another.

Preparation
Oh my! The lawyers might have more of a say in this than I would like. They make me feel like I have to tell you not to use a hair dryer in the shower. If you are that stupid you shouldn't be having sex with another human anyway.

Buy professionally aged meat … buy it the day you are to serve it. It's harder to trash a great cut of meat than a cheap one. You can recover from a middle of the road mistake with Filet Mignon, but flank steak will be an ugly thing to recover from. Boy, it can get tough fast. You don't want to have to eat out in a restaurant. That's failure in the making.

If you have to buy the meat the day before you are to serve it, rinse the meat well with cold fresh water and pat it dry with a paper towel. Wrap it in a cling wrap so no air can get to it. Put it in a dish with more cling wrap to seal the dish from refrigerator spills and odors.

Do not marinate meat more than two hours before cooking. A good steak hardly needs marinating.

Take the meat out of the fridge a couple of hours before you are to cook it. Take it off of the cold dish and put it on a room temperature plate. But leave it in the cling wrap while it sits. Meat marinates and cooks best if it's at room temperature when you start.

In case you missed it the first time:
Never marinate any meat more than two hours.

Also, in case you missed it the first time, ask for help if you need to. Any guy that works in the store will help you with your choices. Be sure to tell him you are doing your best to make a Panty Dropper Meal. They'll pick the best quality produce and meats for you. The produce guy will get you the freshest, crispest produce. The meat cutter at any supermarket will custom-cut small portions of the best-quality meat for you at no extra charge.

Here is the way to start your conversation with the service folks. Use your own words but get this idea across in the first three sentences. *"I need your help. I have invited a really cute young woman over for dinner and I want to make the absolute best meal I can for her. The goal here is to have her empty panties on my bedroom floor overnight."* You'll get the highest quality food and you'll quickly become his favorite customer. Even better, show him the cover of this book. He'll understand instantly.

Generally speaking, all your meats need to be the freshest possible when you're trying to impress.

Chicken, and certainly fish, should be of the highest quality. Fish can be touchy because not everyone likes fish. Once you know her, if you decide you want to cook for her again, go for fish. Stay safe though, on the first date. Chicken is always a safe bet, and if she's a red meat eater, beef will be your best bet. *Nothing tastes better than a well-prepared filet mignon.*

Breakfast In Bed

Find out what kind of breakfast she likes. Unless you are in Texas, where women like "Manly Breakfasts," it could easily be cold yogurt and granola. Boy, I sure hope so, as that is really easy and you can toss in some fresh organic fruit slices too.

I found a wonderful folding-leg beechwood bed tray for $19^{95} on the Internet. No assembly required. Buy a bed tray to keep her naked in bed. Serve her breakfast in bed. Sit on the edge of the bed and share the yogurt and granola so you are ready to put her tray on the floor as soon as she's done. Watch her eat, she'll love the attention. Kiss her, put a little yogurt around a nipple, lick it off, and you're off to the races again.

Guys are tempted to get one in before she escapes in the morning. That's always a good thing, actually, for both of you. You have two choices; either do your best to get up before she does and get her going with yogurt and granola, or an omelet with coffee in bed, or get your morning sex first, then treat her to breakfast. You're likely to get a repeat of the repeat that way. You can go back to sleep after she leaves.

Printable Recipe Pages

Guys, this book is a dead bust if she sees it. You can't have it on the kitchen counter while making a meal; you can't let her see it. Actually, I would prefer that this book is never seen by any woman, but that's not practical.

Bacon-Wrapped Scallops with Jasmine Rice & Baby Spinach Greens

The web site is designed so you can download the recipe, including a picture of what it is supposed to look like when you are finished. Print the recipe so you can work from it in the kitchen without the book being seen.

www.thepantydroppercookbook.com | password: onthefloor

Body Language In The Kitchen

Women are in tune to the non-verbal. You need to have your body square to hers. You want your shoulders square to hers and your hips square to hers. You have to demonstrate that you want her. It isn't obvious, it's subliminal. It will help get the gate guardians to relax their control.

Be A Clown (Or Not)

Being a clown can be fun. It's full of surprises for everyone watching. It's risky on a date, though. Having surprises while naked in the dark won't be high on her list of things she wants you to do with her. At least not on the first date.

Some mistakes are too much fun to only make once.

Safe Sex

This is not just a cookbook. I like to think of it as having recipes for life. I also like to think of it as a hunting book. I can't seem to make up my mind which it is, cooking or hunting.

I don't have anything to say about safe sex. After all the years and all the dialogue and lectures you've heard on this subject, what could I say except BELIEVE THEM!

Safe sex is good. And you don't have to feel that you're missing out by having safe sex. Be creative! I would like to quote one of my favorite people. My doctor says, "If you aren't living on the edge, you're taking up too much space!" Here's wishing you safe sex and lots of it!

There's an old Spanish proverb: "Life is short, very, very short. It's also very, very wide."

Don't look ahead so much as look right and left. There's an amazing amount of room to party, just not a lot of time to party. Believe me, go to the party every chance you get. You don't want to look back on your life from 70 years old and wish you had partied more than you did. Go to the party.

Penis-Shaped Foods

Why are there so many penis-shaped foods? (Don't tell the PC women.) It's starting to look like sex discrimination and I'm getting very afraid. I'm always afraid of the PC women. With PC women it doesn't matter if I'm right or wrong or if they are right or wrong. Once they start talking, I always feel like I'm wrong. WTF is up with that? Maybe to help the PC women with the "food shaped like a penis" issue, we could repackage brats to look like their female counterpart. How about sausages, hot dogs or salamis? Would the repackaged meats fit the BBQ grill better? Maybe.

When the large brats hit the BBQ grill, there are often lots of jokes about "male members." If the meats were shaped "the sexually equal PC way," would it be as funny? What if the meats on the grill were forced to be PC 50/50, male and female? Would there be any jokes in mixed company, or would we just stand around the BBQ grill blinking our eyes and not talking about what we see? If nobody was looking, would you try to fit the grill meats together? *Don't play with your food!*

We men seem to have the same feelings of fear about women in positions of authority. I'm sure that women belong to a collective "we have to control men" conspiracy. Think about this logically and you'll realize mothers induce a mental virus into their male children. Women train each other on how to do this in secret meetings. Girl's Night Out? Not really. Girls Night Out is a secret meeting; it's a plotting session.

If You Are Under Thirty

If you are under thirty, skip these pages.

Here is a subject that you must pay attention to. This can be very important to you. I won't write much about this because it has nothing to do with recipes or hunting for what's hidden in a girl's panties, but it does have a bunch to do with repeat sexual performances.

A few of these recipes are going to work well for you. You will be getting better and better at hunting and making the score. You'll find it is easy to get panties to sit on your bedroom floor overnight and you'll wonder why no one told you how to do this sooner.

Let's say one of the women you invite over is a real standout and you know it from the very beginning of the evening. She is different from the others and you'd like to have her over again and again. This is the one you want to talk to before you fall asleep. Now what? If this part of my book were on Oprah, they would call it "Pillow Talk." I'm sure Oprah could spend an hour on this subject. Dr. Phil would call this a "must do" to develop a lasting relationship. I know you don't watch either show. It's for the best.

Most of us guys would gag on the subject, but here is the one item you must pay attention to if you want her to come back: *Talk to her.* Ask her where she grew up and what it was like there. Don't ask about her family, as there is a good chance she had one of those weird uncles or stepfathers. Family is a taboo subject unless she brings it up. Try talking to her about her city, town or neighborhood. Schools are OK too. "Tell me about your best friend in grade school." If you are really interested in her making a repeat visit, show her that you are interested in her life. She'll realize you want to get to know her and that you are not just interested in what she keeps in the panties she has dropped on your floor. Showing interest is dangerous, as it may be a life-changing direction you are contemplating.

If you are under thirty, don't do it.

If the "conversations in the afterglow" work out, you may find that you have to give this book to your brother, now that he's single again.

Thoughts and Advice

I have a friend who gets more sex than anyone else I know. He isn't a looker by any means. He looks coarse and he acts coarse. You'd think that a matched pair of "coarsenesses" would put him near the bottom of the list of people who get lucky every Saturday night, but he scores every Saturday night. If he starts after work Friday, he scores Friday and Saturday. He's out of the bars and on the way home by ten thirty in the evening. It used to irritate me sometimes that he'd get lucky and I wouldn't. He didn't just get lucky often, he got lucky every time he went out. Finally I couldn't take it anymore and had to ask him how he did it. He simply said, *"It's easy. Just follow my mantra: Go ugly early!"* Personally, I just couldn't do it and his suggestion never improved my sex life. I'm not promoting that you "Go ugly early." However, if you learn from this book how to present a meal to a date, your sex life will

dramatically improve.

Rules
Turn your telephone answering machine on and have it on mute. Turn your cell phone off. If your landline phone has a way to turn off the ring, be sure to do that. The damn phone will ring at exactly the wrong time, every time.

Ask her, *"Unless you are expecting an emergency, could I please ask that you turn your cell phone off? I'd like to have an evening with you without interruptions."* She'll think you are interested in her. You do know, it never fails that at a peak moment, the phone will ring. This is critical; you must understand that the phone gods work against men.

Fight or Flight

Look around in nature. Look at the males. Males are the ones that display, be it colors or dances or prowess. Males work at attracting mates. Showing her that you can feed her and house her gets you sex. You need to show some flurries of color and style to become the one she chooses to mate with tonight. Listen up here, I don't mean show up in a Hawaiian shirt. The kind of color I'm talking about is lifestyle color. You have to make yourself stand out by being different and better than the other mating possibilities for her. It really is that simple.

Food is a great turn on. Why? Because food is colorful and beautiful to look at. Many of the recipes here are designed with multiple colors in mind. Buy a bag of mixed organic greens for a salad. Add your own chopped red, yellow, orange and green bell peppers. These colors are all in one salad for a reason. Colorful food will get you past another of those gate guardians. Newman's Own® Organics dressings are great, with a wide variety of flavors. After taxes, Paul Newman donates all his profits and royalties to various charities. Good organic flavor and all the profits to charity are two strong reasons to buy Newman's Own.®

There are little triggers in the mating area of her brain that you must trip. In some women the triggers are easy to find, and in others they are well guarded. The latter group of women are known as "hard to get." They are still "get-able" though.

You have to find out what it takes to get past the gate guardians to get to the triggers. I suggest food, money and pheromones. You have to have the food, but you don't actually have to have the money. Just appearing sincere about a money plan is all you need. You can talk about going aggressively after a cash goal, a lifestyle. Keep your story within the realm of reality. You won't pass the guardians to the trigger if you go into fantasyland about being "The Donald." Look around. There is only one "The Donald." Don't make your story obvious BS.

Think of all the multi-millionaires that no one has ever heard of. Just offhand, I know of two guys who own many thousands of apartment units each. No one in the national press has ever heard of them. They don't need security guards, but they are worth a billion dollars each. Intriguing! You too could "own" several apartments. Give your story some intrigue. It can be very interesting if, in the telling, you talk about the negotiation or the treasure hunt in finding undervalued property. Be different, but keep it legal. The fantasy of international drug smuggling or money laundering will quickly be seen as BS. If she believes that kind of story, what she'll see in her mind is Federal Prison for your future. The idea of prison ruins the vision of food and housing for her. Her panties will stay up.

Men, this book is for you only.
Keep it hidden. Don't let the women see it, ever. I hate the fact that this book will be out in public where women might see it. It is a "For Men Only" item. That is why this book doesn't say "Panty Dropper" on the spine. It's camouflaged—so while it is in your book stack or on your bookshelf—it won't reveal itself. Some women are going to see it in the book stores. Some will buy it, but only for their brothers, sons and nephews. It's a guy's book. It's not politically correct. I just hope the Politically Correct Police don't start with me. They are such a pain in the ass. I shouldn't have to hide behind the First Amendment, I'm a guy. Guys wrote the First Amendment. Actually, I'm thoroughly convinced guys wrote the bill of rights to protect us from women.

The Declaration of Independence wasn't written for future generations.
It was written to justify why we were splitting from England. By today's standards, 1776 was a male chauvinist pig society. When they wrote, "all men are created equal," they really meant "MEN." This didn't include women, although they were going to be allowed to go along for the ride.

Kamasutra

I find it amazing that modern society has put such taboos on talking about and performing sex.

I would like to suggest the *Kamasutra*. It is widely known as a source of sexual positions. That is such a narrow piece of the book, but it has given the *Kamasutra* the reputation of pornography.

Actually, there are many chapters that don't discuss sex at all. There are chapters on philosophy and making a profit, as well as chapters on being a good member of society. Buy a complete modern translation. It's a good book on life, including sex.

Vision
Remember, the vision you are looking for is a pair of empty panties on the floor next to your bed.

Pent-up hunting/mating urge
It's like the house cat that gets the crazies and tears through the house, using it's claws in the carpet to go around corners at full speed and then attacks a thread laying on the carpet. Guys get that same feeling and act in the same way. It's frustration over not being a successful hunter. You must hunt. It's in your inner core. If guys were getting all the sex they wanted, they probably wouldn't go outside much. They wouldn't have the energy.

Hopefully, many copies of this book are going to be purchased by fathers, to be given to their bachelor sons as gifts. They will be given clandestinely, so Mom doesn't know. If you are a Dad buying for your son, may I suggest you buy online. Don't get caught with this book in your possession. Have it sent directly to your son's address. You really don't want Mom to know you are promoting sex without "true love" for your son.

the
Panty Dropper COOKBOOK

THE RECIPES

Chef Andy, the man responsible for the recipes in this book asked,
"What happens if she's not wearing panties?"
I guess that under that condition this book is null and void.

Remember, she can have nearly any male she wants.
All she has to do is point and say, "OK, you."

She won't do that. She's not like you.
You'll say "OK" to almost any woman.
She's choosy and you are not.

Don't forget the alcohol.

ABOUT THE COOKING WEBCASTS: You will notice that the directions in the webcast and the directions in the book don't always match. Many of the webcasts demonstrate making the dish for one, but you want to cook for two! The printed recipes in this book, and the printable recipes on the web site are for two.

Cooking isn't rigid. It's not like assembling a machine. There are many approaches to achieving the same delicious result. Watch the webcast for the recipe you are going to make a couple of times the day you are going to make the meal. They're short enough to keep your attention, but quite clear. Be flexible. It's OK to be creative in the kitchen—the bedroom, too.

Get Ready To Cook!

Life's uncertain. Wear your Sunday hat on Monday.

It doesn't matter if the economy is good or bad. You still don't want to take her out to dinner.

It's OK if you look a little inept while making her dinner. She'll think it's cute. Being cute while being in service to her gets you automatically past one of the gate guardians.

If you haven't noticed, the spine of this book doesn't have the full title on it. It's designed so it can sit on a shelf or in a stack and not be a bust if your date sees it. I don't want women to ever see this book. You don't either. This is why there is a companion web site. You can go to the web site, view the video once or twice, and download and print the recipe with the picture of what the final meal should look like. The recipes have no reference to the book or the web site, so if she loves the meal, *(I know she will)* and asks for the recipe, you can just give it to her.

The web site requires a password. The password is *onthefloor*. Please don't share the password with people who haven't bought the book. It's a copyright infringement.

www.thepantydroppercookbook.com

Here is a list of recipes. They sound fancy, but are designed to be really easy to prepare. Don't let the names fool you.

1) Caprese Salad

A great light meal for summer.

2) Boiled Artichokes with Lemon-Garlic Butter

A sumptuous favorite with ancient links to aphrodisiac-induced episodes. Make a colorful salad to go with this.

3) Bacon-Wrapped Scallops with Jasmine Rice
& Baby Spinach Greens

Watch the webcast all the way through.

4) Spicy Shrimp & Mesclun Greens

*Mesclun is the proper term for a salad made
of small, tender greens and lettuces—usually
with about 3 weeks of growth. Often you see
it listed on menus as Mesclun Salad.
Translated, it means "salad salad."*

5) Seared Pork Tenderloin with Roasted
Red Potatoes & Tomato Wine Butter Sauce

*A little more involved, but a killer meal.
Watch the webcast a couple of times.*

6) Chicken with Couscous & Broccoli

*This is a nice meal. It should have her heart
pounding about a half hour after you serve it.*

7) Filet Mignon with Garlic Mashers,
Green Beans & Sauce Verde

*A quality meal. Be sure to ask your date
how she likes the filet cooked.
Rare, medium, etc.*

8) Chicken, Seafood, and Bacon Paella

A traditional Spanish dish that is one of the most involved of all the recipes. If you can do this one, you will not be eating breakfast alone.

9) Pasta with Pesto, Sautéed Mushrooms, Fresh Tomatoes & Artichoke Hearts

You will need a food processor for this one. This is a vegetarian dish for those non-carnivorous dates. Vegetarians are cool. They taste great! But you should be mindful of your objective and ask her if she has any food allergies. Sometimes there are reactions to nuts or dairy, and this recipe has both.

10) Chocolate Icebox Cake

A chocolate dessert. This one lulls all the gate guardians into submission.

11) Chile Cheese Egg Dish

The easiest of all the meals. One of the best too. A nice organic, colorful salad is a good accompaniment. Also good for breakfast.

Caprese Salad

This salad will go well with almost any of the recipes in this cookbook. It's easy to make, colorful and classy. A good summer salad.

NEEDS:

2 medium-size tomatoes

2 mozzarella loaves, preferably buffalo mozzarella

4 or 5 leaves of flat leaf basil, Thai basil, or mint basil

1 pinch of kosher salt

Some freshly ground Grains of Paradise or ground pepper

A drizzle of extra virgin olive oil

HOW TO:

Remove the tomato core by cutting the top off the tomatoes. Carefully slice the tomatoes into rounds a little thicker than a quarter inch.

While holding the soft cheese to reinforce it, make your slices about as thick as the tomato slices. Alternate cheese slices and tomato slices in a pinwheel effect around the plate.

Take four or five leaves of fresh flat leaf basil, Thai basil or mint basil. Put them on your cutting board and fold them together lengthwise and julienne them into small pieces. Sprinkle the basil over the tomato and cheese. Add just a pinch of kosher salt, Grains of Paradise or ground pepper, and drizzle with extra virgin olive oil.

Have a bottle of Balsamic vinegar on the dinner table just in case you or your date would like to add some extra flavor.

Boiled Artichokes with Lemon-Garlic Butter

NEEDS:

2 large artichokes, with tops sliced off

2 lemons

1/2 teaspoon red chili flakes (optional)

1 sprig of fresh rosemary or 1 tablespoon dried Italian seasoning

Fresh parsley

Kosher salt

Grains of Paradise or fresh-cracked pepper

1/4 lb unsalted butter (1 stick)

2 cloves fresh garlic, thinly sliced or minced

Fresh red pepper, diced (optional)

*When enjoying this delicacy, one should start by peeling
the leaves from the outside, dipping the meaty side
into the butter, and scraping it off with the front teeth.
Have a spare bowl around for discarded leaves.
Work your way to the choke and then eat the choke.*

HOW TO:

Start by boiling 3-4 quarts of water on high in a large pot. Add a couple pinches of kosher salt to accelerate boiling.

The artichokes will cook through better if you lop off the bottom stem and the top half inch. By holding it from the base and squeezing with the thumb and fingers, you can get it done with a sharp knife. Watch your fingers.

After the water starts to boil, add a sprig of rosemary or a tablespoon of dried Italian seasoning, one sliced garlic clove and the juice from half a lemon. Add a few dashes of Grains of Paradise or pepper, and red chili flakes (optional). Submerge the artichokes in the water with tongs to avoid a steam burn. Make sure they are placed in with the stem side down. You can use a glass plate to help them stay down. Cover and boil on medium-high for about 20 to 30 minutes.

Just before the artichoke is done, put about a half stick of butter in a small bowl along with one clove of thinly sliced garlic. Place in microwave oven for about 30 seconds. Microwave ovens differ in cooking times so just be sure you don't overheat the butter. You want it melted, not burned.

When checking to see if the choke is done, place it with the top down (stem side up), take a steak knife and poke into the bottom of the stem about an inch. If the knife slides back out easily, they are done. (Another way to check is to pull off one of the outside leaves and see if they easily come off.)

On a cutting board, hold the choke firmly and with the lopped-off part facing down, slice in half with a sharp, non-serrated chef knife. Make sure you are applying pressure to the sides while cutting or it will fall apart. When done, you will see a thick-based choke with concentric leaves that get smaller towards the center where there are spiny hairs. Cut those out with a paring knife. Make sure to remove all the spines and inner leaves, but do not lose the outside leaves or the precious, meaty choke. Pour the butter and garlic into a little bowl or ramekin and toss in a pinch of salt, some chopped parsley, a pinch of Grains of Paradise and the juice from half a squeezed lemon. Stir a bit and place in the center of a large plate. Arrange the halved artichokes (now carved out) around the butter with hollowed side facing up. Squeeze some lemon over each, along with a couple sprinkles of parsley, Italian herbs or Herbs de Provence, and salt. Place a lemon wedge by each half artichoke. Sprinkle some diced red bell pepper on the plate and around the chokes for some color. It's an added touch of color that will be appreciated.

Bacon-Wrapped Scallops with Jasmine Rice & Baby Spinach Greens

NEEDS:

1 bag baby spinach, trimmed and rinsed

8 diver scallops (silver dollar-sized)

8 strips bacon, applewood-smoked or regular

8 toothpicks

1 cup jasmine rice

1 cup chicken or vegetable stock (plus 1 cup water)

1 bottle Tiger Sauce

2 lemon wedges

Grains of Paradise or pepper

2 tablespoons balsamic vinegar

Cooking oil

Small amount of fresh chopped Herbes de Provence
(parsley, rosemary & thyme) to garnish

HOW TO:

Lay the bacon strips flat on a non-stick sheet pan and put in an oven set at 300 degrees for 5 minutes to render out some of the fat. Remove and allow to cool. *(This first step isn't in the webcast, but it's a good idea.)*

Boil one cup of chicken stock and one cup of water in a medium-sized saucepan. The basic rule is two cups boiling water and stock to one cup of rice. Two to one.

Rinse one cup of uncooked rice to remove some of the starches. Add it to your now boiling chicken stock. Stir briefly. Cover and reduce heat to low or simmer. Do not lift lid for at least 8-10 minutes (or until directions on box say so!)

Scallops: On a cutting board, lay the bacon flat. Roll the scallop up in the bacon until it overlaps itself by at least 1/4 inch. Take a toothpick and poke it through the meatiest part of that overlap. Continue skewering, keeping as centered as possible, straight through. Do this for all 8 scallops.

Heat a fry pan on high and add two tablespoons of cooking oil. Sprinkle salt and Grains of Paradise over 4 scallops and add to pan. Be careful of oil splatters. Allow to cook on each side for four to six minutes per side, giving them a golden brown color. DO NOT BLACKEN! Remove from the skillet and place them on the sheet pan and repeat the process with the remaining 4 scallops. When all 8 scallops are properly seared, place them in the oven for an additional 3-5 minutes. *(Finishing the scallops in the oven isn't in the webcast, but it will assure the scallops are cooked through and warm when served.)*

The rice will be finishing up about the same time as the scallops, so we'll start constructing our plates. The spinach should be small leaf, small-stemmed and cleaned. Place a handful in the center of each plate. Drizzle a little balsamic vinegar over the greens. Sprinkle salt and Grains of Paradise as well.

Lightly pack rice into a small bowl or ramekin and drop directly on top of spinach in the center of the plate. Get scallops from oven, gently slide out the toothpicks, and place on the border of the spinach and rice. Drizzle a small amount of Tiger Sauce over each scallop and some of the rice. Lightly sprinkle rice with salt, Grains of Paradise, parsley, thyme, rosemary, and add a lemon wedge to the side of the plate.

If a dipping sauce is desired, combine Tiger Sauce, lemon juice, and mayonnaise in a small bowl and serve as an accompaniment.

Spicy Shrimp and Mesclun Greens

Mesclun is the proper term for a salad made of small, tender greens and lettuces-usually with about 3 weeks of growth. Often you see it listed on menus as Mesclun Salad. Translated, it means *salad salad*.

NEEDS:

1/4 lb. bag fresh mesclun greens

10-12 shrimp, size 26/30 per pound, peeled and deveined with tail on

2 kiwis, sliced and skinned

10 grape or cherry tomatoes

2 grapefruit, cleaned of seeds and pith, cut into wedges

1 avocado

1 cucumber

2 lemon wedges

1 lime

1 small can water chestnuts *(optional)*

Olive oil

Soy sauce

Seasoned rice vinegar

Sweet chili sauce for seafood *(Nam Ploi is a good brand)*

A pinch of cilantro, chopped

Grains of Paradise *(optional)*

HOW TO:

Marinate shrimp for half an hour to an hour in soy sauce, sweet chili sauce, and a little bit of rice vinegar.

The slicing of the fruit and avocado for this dish can be seen in action on the webcast. They should be prepared in advance of executing the rest of this dish and put aside. If one were bold enough, slice them in front of your guest while waiting for the fry pan to heat up to high.

Using your fingers, sort through the mesclun greens to pick out any undesirable leaves or possible dirt, and place two good handfuls in a salad spinner and wash with cold water. Spin. Distribute the greens evenly across the two plates and lightly sprinkle with rice vinegar and soy sauce. Toss a bit and begin adding sliced grape tomatoes, sliced cucumbers grapefruit, kiwi, and avocado scoops over the top. Carrots, radish sprouts, water chestnuts and red peppers would also go great tossed in with this dish. Throw in a few pinches of salt and Grains of Paradise.

Once the pan is hot, add 2 tablespoons of olive or vegetable oil and keep on high until oil begins to smoke. Toss in shrimp and watch out for oil splatters. Distribute shrimp evenly across the pan and keep on high for another 1 ½ to 2 minutes. Sprinkle salt and Grains of Paradise on each and then turn over with tongs. Shrimp should be bright pink with shades of golden brown from frying.

When bringing the shrimp onto the salad, be creative. The janitors of the sea deserve a parade; so arrange them like synchronized swimmers. For the dressing, drizzle some sweet chili sauce, a touch of soy sauce, a pinch of cilantro and a squirt of lime juice. Serve with a lemon wedge on the side.

Seared Pork Tenderloin with Roasted Red Potatoes & Tomato Wine Butter Sauce

NEEDS:

Meat thermometer

1 1½ - 2 lb. pork tenderloin

4 small red potatoes with skins on, washed, cut into eighths

2 green onions, sliced

1 clove garlic, sliced

4 pinches fresh ginger, minced

1 cup stewed tomatoes, drained

Fresh chopped parsley

2/3 cup dry white wine

4 tablespoons unsalted butter

1/3 cup canola oil for browning pork

Olive oil for potatoes (to taste)

For Pork Rub, combine:

1 cup dry bread crumbs

2 tablespoons paprika

2 tablespoons dried mustard powder

2 tablespoons Grains of Paradise or fresh cracked pepper

2 tablespoons kosher salt

1 tablespoon garlic powder*

*In the webcast, Chef Andy says "garlic salt." Use garlic powder so you don't double salt the pork.

HOW TO:

Preheat oven to 350 degrees.

POTATOES: Put eighth-cut potatoes in a mixing bowl, drizzle a liberal amount of olive oil over them, add a couple of pinches of parsley (or any of your favorite herbs), 2 teaspoons kosher salt and some Grains of Paradise. Toss well, distributing throughout, and spread out evenly, skin side down, on a rimmed cookie sheet. Put into oven and set timer for 25 minutes.

PORK: Remove the pork tenderloin from plastic wrap and pat dry with a paper towel. Put pork rub mixture on a plate, and begin by rolling the tenderloin in the mixture so it covers the entire piece of meat. Next, get a fry pan on the range top and heat on high. Pour 1/3 cup oil into the pan and wait for it to get smoking. Put the whole tenderloin into the pan, being mindful of oil splatters, and let cook for about 2-3 minutes on each side. You may need to turn the heat down a bit so the meat doesn't burn. You want to sear the outside all the way around, thus fusing all the juices inside. Keep rotating with tongs to sear all sides. The tenderloin should have a golden-brown hue all around. When this is done, remove the tenderloin and turn heat to medium. DO NOT DISCARD PAN JUICES. *(If there's a lot of oil, you can carefully spoon off some of it and discard. The brown bits left in the pan will add great flavor to the sauce you will make next.)*

Put the pork in the oven with the potatoes. There should still be 15-20 minutes left on the oven timer.

SAUCE: The webcast is slightly different. Chef Andy starts with butter instead of the pan juices. This paragraph is a more flavorful way to make it. With the fry pan on medium or medium-high, add minced green onions, ginger and garlic to the reserved pan juices and stir for 2 minutes, releasing their aromas. Add tomatoes. Cook for 2-3 minutes, then add white wine. Immediately reduce heat to low/simmer and leave alone to let the wine reduce, leaving you with a nice combo of sweet and salty. Taste it, and if you want a little more richness, add some butter.

You should have a couple of minutes here, so now would be a good time to do a little cleanup.

When timer is up, pull out the potatoes and arrange them in the center of the plates.

Take the pork out of the oven. Insert a stem thermometer into the thick end of the side of the tenderloin and look for an inside temperature of 150-160 degrees. Pork is usually served at 165 degrees, but it will keep cooking itself for a few more minutes. On a cutting board, bias slice the tenderloin into medallions about one-half inch thick and drape the pork across the potatoes.

Finish off by drizzling the tomato wine butter sauce over all. Top off with a little bit of parsley. Add salt and pepper to taste.

Chicken with Couscous & Broccoli

NEEDS:

1 box dried couscous (preferably lemon, herb & garlic)

1 small box sun-dried currants

2 trimmed and cleaned 8 oz. chicken breasts

1 16 oz. can vegetable or chicken stock

1 tablespoon extra virgin olive oil

1 small jar Spanish olives (stuffed with pimentos)

1 head of broccoli, stemmed (cut into small florets)

1 small can or jar of whole roasted red peppers

6 slices of French baguette, toasted with Parmesan cheese

1 teaspoon minced garlic or garlic powder

2 tablespoons butter

1 small pinch smoky paprika

HOW TO:

For the couscous, empty contents of the box and spice pack into a bowl or 6 x 9" Pyrex dish. Using directions on the couscous box, put half water and half chicken or vegetable stock instead of all water into a saucepan. Mix in one tablespoon of olive oil. Bring to a slow boil. Pour the prescribed amount of simmered stock and water over the couscous. Sprinkle a small handful of sun-dried currants over the top. *(Chef Andy forgot to add them at this point in the webcast, but he likes them for the flavor dimension they add.)* Cover tightly with plastic wrap and set aside.

Broccoli: In another pot, boil 1 quart of water and ½ teaspoon salt. Lop the broccoli floret off from the stem and cut the floret into bite-size pieces. Next, drop the broccoli into the boiling water. Keep the water at a high boil for about two minutes and then reduce to a low and slow boil or it will overcook.

Chicken: Butterfly cut the chicken breasts. *(Watch the webcast and pay special attention to the part about cross-contamination.)* In a fry pan or skillet, heat a couple of tablespoons of vegetable oil on medium high. Season one side of the chicken breasts and drop into pan, seasoned side down. Season the other side. Be careful of hot oil splatters. Cook for about 2 minutes, until side is golden brown. Turn over and reduce heat to medium-low. Add 7 or 8 pimento olives that have been cut in half and some sliced roasted red peppers. Also add 2 tablespoons of butter to infuse the flavors in the pan.

The broccoli is now cooked enough. Look for a crisp texture and a bright green hue. Remove from heat and place in bowl.

Remove wrap from couscous and fluff with a fork. Then place a moderate amount on right side of the plate. Pull chicken breasts from the pan and slice across with chef knife, creating quarter-inch slices. Place 4 or 5 broccoli pieces on the side of the plate.

Spoon olives, red peppers and juice over the chicken, broccoli and couscous, but don't drown it! If you have any Parmesan cheese still around, it could be sprinkled

over the broccoli. Toasted baguette is suggested as an accompaniment if you are looking to soak up all that delicious sauce on your plate.

Filet Mignon with Garlic Mashers, Green Beans & Sauce Verde

This is a great dish for a traditional kind of date—meat 'n' potatoes. The green beans with Sauce Verde (*verde* is Spanish for *green*) will add an element of zest to it all. If there is an issue about the garlic causing bad breath, then speak up in its defense about the therapeutic, homeopathic qualities it has, in addition to the awesome flavor it contributes to a meal. Garlic breath won't be an issue if you both have garlic.

This is a "busy to make" meal. I suggest you try making this one at least once before you invite a date over.

NEEDS:

For the Sauce Verde:

3 sprigs of fresh mint, with stems removed and chopped fine

1/2 bunch of fresh Italian (flat leaf) parsley, stemmed and chopped fine

1/3 cup of extra virgin olive oil

1 teaspoon kosher salt

1/2 lemon, squeezed (*Not in the webcast, but it enhances the flavor. Use it.*)

OTHER INGREDIENTS:

2 8-10 oz. prime-cut filet mignon steaks *(Tell your local butcher what you have in mind and he will steer you in the right direction.)*

8 red potatoes, skin on, cut into quarters

1/2 cup heavy whipping cream

1/2 stick unsalted butter (4 tablespoons)

1/2 lb. fresh green beans, stemmed, tips on

2 cloves fresh garlic, minced or sliced thin

Herbes de Provence (parsley, rosemary, thyme)

Kosher salt

Grains of Paradise or fresh cracked pepper

1 package instant gravy for beef

Caramelized onions *(Optional; sauté onions in olive oil until caramel colored)*

HOW TO:

Get the filets out early. About an hour before you start to cook, pull the filets out of the fridge, put them on a room-temperature plate, and leave uncovered. You want to bring them gradually up to room temperature before grilling. This will ensure even cooking throughout. Otherwise the center of the filets can be too rare.

Start the potatoes: Set the oven for 375 degrees and get a cookie sheet pan ready. Put the quartered potatoes in a mixing bowl and add a couple tablespoons of olive oil, a teaspoon of salt, a teaspoon of fresh cracked pepper, and a pinch of Herbs de Provence. Mix well, making sure the potatoes are thoroughly draped with oil. Lay out evenly on the cookie sheet pan with the skin side down, and place them in the oven uncovered. They will take 10-15 minutes. *(This step is not in the webcast, but roasting gives more flavor depth.)*

If serving gravy, follow the instructions on the packet and begin it now. Add a small amount of caramelized onions and Herbes de Provence. After it's made, stir your gravy every few minutes. Don't let a skin form on the surface from dehydration.

For the Sauce Verde, finely chop the mint and parsley. In a small bowl, add this to about 1/3 cup of extra virgin olive oil and the juice from half a small lemon. Add a pinch of salt and some ground Grains of Paradise or freshly ground black pepper and give it a good mix. Cover with plastic wrap and set aside.

When potatoes are soft and slightly golden in hue, pull them from the oven and place in a saucepan. Put heat on medium-low and add 4 tablespoons of butter, half a cup of heavy cream, a couple pinches of salt, some pepper, and Herbes de Provence. Stir occasionally. *Turn the page. The extra effort for this meal will be worth it!*

Filet Mignon with Garlic Mashers,
Green Beans & Sauce Verde
(CONTINUED)

Start heating a pan on high for the filet mignon. Use a cast-iron skillet. If none is available, then a stainless steel or Teflon-coated fry pan will do.

Boil water for the green beans. Fill a 4-quart pot halfway with water and add a good pinch of kosher salt. Salt enhances the green color of the beans. You will want to drop them into the boiling water about 5 minutes before the steak and potatoes are done because that's how quickly they cook.

For the filet mignon: With the heat still on high, add a couple tablespoons of extra virgin olive oil. Dress the filets with a drizzle of extra virgin olive oil, salt and pepper. When pan is smoking hot, drop the seasoned side of the filets down first in the pan, season the other side, and leave alone for 3-5 minutes to nicely sear. Turn them over and continue cooking for another 3-5 minutes.

The webcast says 6 minutes per side. This is only correct if you have a very thick filet. I like 3 minutes, but then again, I like mine very rare. Most people like them cooked a little closer to medium. Once again, cooking isn't cast in stone. After 4 minutes per side, cut one open and look. It's OK to look. If done enough, put the steaks on a plate, cover loosely with a "tent" made with aluminum foil. This will keep the steaks warm while you cook the beans and finish up the potatoes. Keep the foil tent loose or it will hold too much heat and your steaks may end up overcooked.

Your beans are ready for cooking. Drop them into the boiling water. Cover and put on medium-high.

Now, your potatoes should be finishing up. When the steaks have been flipped and are close to done, pour the potato and cream mixture from the pan into a mixing bowl. Add a little bit of minced (or thinly sliced) garlic, and a tablespoon of butter. Mash with a whisk, masher, or fork. It's OK if they're a little lumpy. Place a serving on each plate and sprinkle another pinch of herbs over the top.

Remove the beans from the boiling water and shake off the excess water. They should be *al dente*, which means a little on the crispy side. Place them on your dinner plates. Mix the Sauce Verde and spoon it over the green beans. Drizzle some around the rim of the plate for a visual effect.

Serve the steak. Ask her if she would like you to cut the meat for her. If so, grab the tongs, and, with a chef knife, slice the meat into thin slices (about a quarter-inch thick). Fan out the slices on top of a little of the gravy. Spoon some gravy on top of the potatoes and serve.

Note: Sometimes it can make a positive difference to preheat the plates that you will be serving by turning the oven on to low (200 degrees) and warming them up for 5 minutes before plate-up. This way, food won't cool off so quickly and y'all can put more energy into talking or something.

Chicken, Seafood & Bacon Paella

A traditional Spanish dish, this paella is one of the most involved of all the recipes. If you can do this one, you will not be eating breakfast alone. *Watch the webcast all the way through a couple of times.*

NEEDS:

1 cup short-grain rice, such as arborio

1 cup canned stewed tomatoes, drained of water

4 slices bacon, chopped

2 cups vegetable or chicken stock

2/3 cup dry white wine, like Riesling

1 small can or jar roasted red peppers (optional)

1 yellow onion, medium dice

2 teaspoons minced garlic

1/2 cup frozen green peas, thawed

16 or so manila clams or steamer clams (roughly the size of a half-dollar)

12 medium-size shrimp (26/30 per pound is the ideal size)

2 small chicken breasts, thinly sliced

Small pinch of saffron (8-10 stamens)

Herbes de Provence (parsley, rosemary, thyme)

HOW TO:

Heat a large fry pan or cast iron skillet to medium-high. Add chopped bacon, sliced chicken breast and diced onion. Let those cook together, allowing juices to mingle, for about 10 minutes, stirring frequently.

Add to the pan: saffron, white wine and garlic. *(I know, the garlic didn't make it into the webcast. Add it here).* Reduce heat to low. Add one cup rice to pan with 1½ cups of vegetable or chicken stock. Stir frequently for the first minute.

Scatter clams, shrimp, and stewed tomatoes over the rice. Keep heat on low, cover with lid and LEAVE IT ALONE. Rice should take about 10 more minutes to cook through, and in turn it will cook the seafood.

Near the end of the cooking time, check to make sure the clams are open. Throw the unopened ones away! *They will make you sick.*

Add the peas, roasted red peppers and a little bit of Herbs de Provence.

Check to make sure rice is finished cooking. Begin plating by moving the seafood and chicken to one edge of the pan. Begin scooping the rice mixture from the bottom of the pan onto your plate and then covering the rice with your seafood, chicken, bacon, and veggies. At the table, add salt and pepper to taste.

Pasta with Pesto, Sautéed Mushrooms, Fresh Tomatoes & Artichoke Hearts

This is a vegetarian dish for those non-carnivorous dates. Vegetarians are cool. They taste great! But you should be mindful of your objective and ask her if she has any food allergies. Often there are reactions to nuts or dairy, and this dish has both.

NEEDS:

1 lb. penne, spaghetti, linguini, or angel hair pasta

2 large portobello mushrooms, stems removed

1 small can of artichoke hearts, drained of water

8-10 vine-ripened cherry tomatoes, sliced in half

1/4 cup white wine (like Chardonnay)

Grains of Paradise

Red chili flakes (optional)

For the pesto:

1 bunch fresh basil, stemmed *(do not use dried basil)*, washed in cold water

2 cloves fresh garlic, sliced thin

1 cup pine nuts, walnuts or hazelnuts (unsalted)

1 cup extra virgin olive oil

1 teaspoon kosher salt

1/2 lemon, squeezed

3/4 cup fresh parmesan cheese, shredded, plus additional for garnishing the dish

HOW TO:

About an hour before you start cooking remove the stems from the two portobello mushrooms and place bottom side up in a bowl. Drizzle olive oil and balsamic vinegar over each mushroom and let marinate for an hour.

For the pesto: You will need a food processor for this part, such as a Cuisinart. Start by throwing in the nuts, garlic, basil and about three pinches of salt. Whizz it up on high while slowly drizzling about five or six tablespoons of extra virgin olive oil. Open up and scrape down the sides of the bowl with a rubber spatula. Next, add the Parmesan cheese and juice from half a lemon. When you turn the processor back on, SLOWLY drizzle the rest of the olive oil into the opening on the top and watch for all to blend into a grainy/creamy paste. Scrape down the sides again and make sure there are no large chunks in the pesto. It should be bright green with white grains and not too oily or runny. Transfer to a non-stainless steel bowl. Glass or plastic is best, and cover tightly with plastic wrap. If you don't, then the basil will oxidize and turn brown. Put it aside.

Get a large stock pot filled with 4-6 quarts of water for the pasta and turn burner on high. In this case, we'll use penne pasta, the kind that looks like one-inch cylinders. When the water is at a rolling boil, toss in the pasta and stir well, making sure none of the penne clumps together. Bring back to a boil and set heat on medium. It will need about eleven minutes to cook. Use your timer. *Watch the webcast to learn how to check to see when it's done.*

While waiting for the water to boil, get a fry pan on medium and add 2 tablespoons of extra virgin olive oil. Slice the mushrooms into large strips, add a pinch of Grains of Paradise or ground black pepper. Cook mushrooms about 5 minutes, until they turn dark brown and shrink. Add the white wine. (*I know, we missed the white wine in the webcast. It's OK, add the white wine here.*) During this break, do a little cleanup.

With 3 minutes to go, add artichoke hearts to the mushrooms and keep heat on low.

When time is up, test a piece of pasta by biting into it. It should be cooked all the way through, with no toughness or leathery texture. Drain into a colander. Add the pasta to the bowl with the pesto. Stir the penne gently into the pesto with the rubber spatula, getting an even distribution through all. Add the tomatoes and stir gently. Don't mangle it. Serve in a large bowl and top with the mushrooms and artichokes, but do not pour in too much wine from the pan. If you want a little zing, add just a touch of red chili flake. Salt and pepper to taste. You can top with some grated Parmesan cheese if you like.

Chocolate Icebox Cake

This is a low-maintenance, low-calorie dessert that shows one's ability to improvise with common, everyday ingredients. Since it will be served in a clear glass, *BE NEAT*. Let your guest see the layers of your offering.

NEEDS:

1 box Jello®-brand instant pudding, chocolate flavor

1 pint milk

1/2 pint heavy whipping cream *(ready-made Cool Whip® optional)*

1/4 cup sugar

2 bananas

1 box Nilla Wafers®

Fresh strawberries (optional)

Fresh mint leaf (optional)

2 large martini or decorative clear goblet-style glasses

HOW TO:

First, the pudding must be mixed and refrigerated for the time needed to thicken up. Follow the instructions on the box. If you are making the whipped cream, then whip the half pint with the sugar until it becomes stiff.

Peel bananas and slice into quarter-inch medallions. When assembling the dish, layer the Nilla Wafers first, the bananas next, followed by a healthy layer of pudding. Try to repeat the layers at least twice, ending up with the top having wafers showing and bananas showing. Top with whipped cream.

For a nice touch, serve with strawberries on the side.

If all goes as planned, she'll be joining you for breakfast.
Turn the page for a make-ahead recipe that will satisfy your hunger
in the morning. You're both going to need a hearty breakfast!

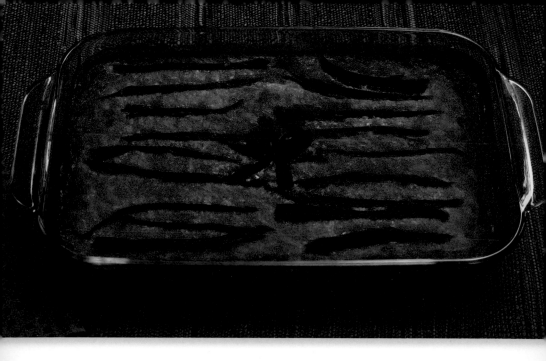

Chile Cheese Egg Dish

This dish makes a lot. Warmed in the microwave it will make a great breakfast the following day, served with fruit, sausages or just plain toast. It can last up to about four days in the fridge. *This recipe is so easy, we didn't even bother to do a webcast for it!*

NEEDS:

5 eggs

1 pint whipping cream

1 can whole Ortega chilies, cut into thin strips

8 oz. grated cheddar cheese

8 oz. grated Jack cheese

Roasted or fresh red pepper for garnishing

HOW TO:

Turn on oven to 350 degrees. Spread Ortega chilies in 9 x 13" Pyrex dish, reserving some to garnish the top as shown in the photo.

Reserve about 2 tablespoons of cheddar and two tablespoons of Jack. Mix all the other ingredients together in a bowl and whisk. Pour over the chilies in the Pyrex dish. Top it with reserved cheeses and chilies.

Bake at 350 degrees for about a half hour or until it is cooked. Test by inserting a sharp knife. It should come out clean. Add some sliced or chopped roasted red pepper and cilantro or fresh parsley to add some color on top. Serve warm.

Thanks

I like to give credit where credit is due. Donny Deutsch was the inspiration for this book. *The Big Idea*, his tv show on CNBC, is a treat to watch. The show is about your finding an item that is missing from the lives of many people and manufacturing that item for commercial sale. He has said many times, and I'm paraphrasing here, "Look for something that is missing in your life and decide if it is missing in other people's lives too. You may have a *Big Idea* of your own in the making."

I couldn't think of anything to manufacture that I didn't already have. I couldn't think of anything that would make my life or your lives better or easier. *The one thing that was missing in my life was sex, more sex.* I know every man would like more sex. How could I help my fellow men achieve more sex? *The Panty Dropper Cookbook* was born.

I'd like to thank my wife Helen and my son Luke for the art work.
My son Jesse for proofreading.

Danny Toback doesn't even know, but his early encouragement kept me on task.

Pam Lemelin for all the aesthetic assembly of the book and the art.
She made it beautiful.

Brett Paine and Magic Hour Films in Seattle for brilliantly editing the web cast videos.

Chris Towey for his camera talent and the
Towey family for the generous use of their home.

Chef Andy Simard for his recipes, his gift as a chef and his talent on camera.

Ann Freeman for being such a help with the production of the videos.

Rob Cook for his computer and internet genius.

Thanks to Sonja Woods, whose wonderful legs grace the cover of this book.

LUKE DODGE